Spotlight on Reading

Summarizing

Grades 5–6

Frank Schaffer

An imprint of Carson-Dellosa Publishing LLC
Greensboro, North Carolina

Credits

Layout and Cover Design: Van Harris
Development House: The Research Masters

Cover Photo: Image Copyright Kiselev Andrey Valerevich, 2011 Used under license from Shutterstock.com

 This book has been correlated to state, common core state, national, and Canadian provincial standards. Visit *www.carsondellosa.com* to search for and view its correlations to your standards.

Frank Schaffer
An imprint of Carson-Dellosa Publishing LLC
PO Box 35665
Greensboro, NC 27425 USA
www.carsondellosa.com

ISBN 978-16-099-6497-9
03-119137784

About the Book

Summarizing is the skill of comprehending, focusing on important information, and rephrasing that information in a concise form. *Summarizing* for grades 5–6 contains guided activities that help develop and achieve this skill. As this skill is practiced in reading, students will naturally begin to use the skill in writing and speaking. Summarization is a concept used throughout the curriculum. Social studies, science, language, and reading all use the skill of summarization in written, reading, and oral lessons.

This book provides activities that will give students the opportunity to discuss, examine, choose, and write summaries. It will also provide the chance to practice using active verbs, and colorful, interesting nouns in their work.

• •

Table of Contents

War Heroes

Read these passages about three heroes of World War II. Circle the best summary for each passage.

• •

Charles de Gaulle was a French general in the Second World War. When France was invaded by the German army, he escaped to London. While in exile, he formed the French Free Forces. He encouraged the French people to resist the German army. This led to the creation of the French Resistance. Charles de Gaulle continued to lead the French people in their fight for freedom for their nation, until the war ended. He later became the president of France.

1. Which sentence best summarizes the passage above?
    a. Charles de Gaulle was known for his determination.
    b. Charles de Gaulle helped create the French Resistance.
    c. Charles de Gaulle became the president of France.

Virginia Hall was an American living in France during World War II. She had lost her leg several years earlier and wore a wooden prosthetic. Although her wooden leg sometimes made it difficult to get around, she was determined to help stop the Germans. Hall helped train Resistance fighters. She established safe houses. She hid pilots whose planes had been damaged. She also gathered information. To protect her identity, Hall used a code name. Her efforts saved many lives. After the war, she received an award for her heroic service.

2. Which sentence best summarizes the passage above?
    a. Virginia Hall was recognized for her heroic service.
    b. People with physical disabilities can do many things.
    c. Virginia Hall worked for the Resistance during World War II.

Bernard Montgomery was the best-known British general in World War II. He was commander of the British army. He and his troops served in Africa during the war. Nicknamed "Monty," he gave the German army its first defeat in North Africa. Winston Churchill believed the victory turned the tide of the war. Montgomery later led troops in Europe. He continued to fight until the war ended.

3. Which sentence best summarizes the passage above?
    a. Bernard Montgomery was a British general who fought in Africa.
    b. General Montgomery was nicknamed "Monty."
    c. Bernard Montgomery was friends with Winston Churchill.

Name This Passage!

Read the passage. Circle the best title for the passage.

• •

Scientists use theories to explain the world. A theory is an opinion. To create a theory, scientists first collect facts. They observe, experiment, and share what they find. Then they write a theory that fits their findings. The theory puts it all together.

Long ago, most people thought that the sun moved around Earth. This theory was developed by an early scientist named Ptolemy. Hundreds of years later, another scientist came up with a new theory. An astronomer named Copernicus observed the sky very carefully. He began to notice new things. He changed the old theory to fit his new observations. His new theory stated that the planets actually move around the sun. His theory still stands today.

Scientists continue to come up with new theories. For example, they collect information from fossils to learn more about dinosaurs. Scientists used to think dinosaurs were cold-blooded reptiles. Now, some believe they were too active to be cold-blooded. That would have made them like the lizards of today. Scientists think dinosaurs might have been warm-blooded instead. That is much more like today's birds.

Scientists have changed other theories too. They used to think that *Tyrannosaurus rex* was a scavenger. They thought this dinosaur tracked down dead animals for food. Now, they believe the *T. rex* was a fierce hunter. The dinosaur most likely chased down prey.

Observations support theories. However, theories are not facts. They are informed opinions. These opinions help us understand our world.

1. Copernicus Theories: Fact or Opinion?

2. Watching the Skies

3. What Are Scientific Theories?

4. Life Among the Dinosaurs

A Winter Adventure

Read the passage. Circle the best summary.

● ●

Would you like to vacation on a warm, tropical island? Or would you prefer a more unusual adventure? Try visiting the SnowCastle in Finland. This unusual hotel is made mainly out of snow and ice. When summer comes, the snow and ice thaw, so, a new hotel is built each winter! The first snow castle was built in 1996.

More than 600,000 guests from around the world have given the SnowCastle a try. It offers a great time for children and adults alike. You can sit in snow-covered restaurants and sip warm cocoa. You can visit the art gallery to view the ice sculptures on display. Special light effects highlight their beauty. Also, look out for the Northern Lights. This natural light show flashes vibrant colors in the night sky.

The hotel has fifteen to twenty rooms. Each one is a unique work of art created by a different designer. The SnowCastle also has towers, a chapel for weddings, and a gift shop. There is even a giant snow slide.

Building starts in December and it takes about five weeks to finish. A completed SnowCastle opens in late January. In the spring, the days lengthen, but weather remains frosty. So, you can even visit the SnowCastle during spring break. It is open for business well into April.

Summary A

The first SnowCastle was built in 1996. It is located in the country of Finland. The hotel itself offers fifteen to twenty rooms. Each room is created by a different designer.

Summary B

The SnowCastle is an unusual tourist destination. It is made out of snow and ice. Thousands of visitors come each year to enjoy its hotel, restaurants, art gallery, and other attractions.

Summary C

The Northern Lights can be seen from the SnowCastle. This is a natural light show that appears in the sky. In the night, you can see flashes of vibrant color.

Name _____

Fireflies

Read the passage. Use words from the word bank to complete a summary.

. . . .

> **Word Bank**
>
> hatch   adults   insects
>
> chemicals   mate   light

Fireflies are bioluminescent insects. That means they produce their own light. They do this by combining chemicals in their bodies. When the chemicals mix with oxygen, fireflies light up the rear parts of their bodies.

The purpose of this light is to help the firefly find a mate. Each species of firefly has a special code. The code is made up of a pattern of light. It includes the number and length of flashes and the time between flashes. It also includes the flight pattern while flashing.

After mating, the female firefly lays about 100 eggs. When the eggs hatch, larvae emerge. The larvae are bioluminescent. They are sometimes called glowworms. The larvae eat during the spring, summer, and autumn months. They sleep through two winters. Then, they progress into the next stage of their lives. They crawl into the soil, where they metamorphose, or change, into pupas. After about two months, they emerge as adult fireflies.

Firefly light is not hot. It is, however, very bright. In some countries, fireflies are used as lanterns. People also release fireflies at festivals. It is fun to watch their bright lights flash in the night sky.

Fireflies are bioluminescent _____ . They mix _____

to produce _____ . That helps fireflies to find a _____ .

After mating, the females lay about a hundred eggs. The eggs _____

and larvae emerge. The larvae go through different stages until they

become _____ .

What Is Going On?

Match these summaries with the stories below. Complete the activity on page 9.

● ●

_____ 1. When we help others selflessly, we grow emotionally.

_____ 2. Some fears may often seem to be irrational.

_____ 3. Sights, tastes, or smells may trigger memories of past experiences.

_____ 4. With hard work and determination, we can overcome obstacles.

a. I do not like mice. I know they are just little animals that cannot hurt me. However, mice petrify me. I do not recall any incident or dream that would cause this fear. I do not even remember ever seeing a live mouse, except in a pet shop. But every time someone even mentions that one may be nearby, I climb on a chair and yell, "Mouse!"

b. Mark wanted to go to the park with his friends. But he had promised to walk his neighbor's dog, Riley. Mrs. Conti had had an accident and would not be able to walk for several weeks. Mark thought it would be easy to help her out and walk her dog. He was mistaken. Whatever direction Mark walked, Riley pulled the opposite way. Sometimes, Riley would just sit and refuse to budge. Maybe he is not stubborn but only sad, Mark thought as he sat next to Riley. "It's okay, Riley. Mrs. Conti will be better soon." Riley's brown eyes stared at Mark as if he understood every word. Mark smiled and scratched Riley behind the ears. It felt nice to help out.

c. Terry sniffed and caught the scent of corn roasting on the neighbor's grill. The aroma reminded him of his time at camp last summer. Terry treasured his memories of hiking in the woods, canoeing, and swimming in the cool, crystal waters of the lake. He had met some of his closest friends at camp. Terry reached for the telephone. It had been a long time since he talked with any of his friends from camp. But, now seemed like an excellent time!

d. Kami was excited to become the newest member of the track and field team. But she was worried about it, too. Although she loved to run, hurdling made her nervous. One wrong move, and ouch! She told the coach about her concerns. Coach Girard assured her that she would not learn how to hurdle overnight. But, with hard work and practice, she would soon be hurdling like a champ. Kami took the coach's advice. Before she knew it, she could jump over hurdles with confidence and agility.

5. Write a story that is based on the picture below. Match this summary statement: "People often want what they do not have, but when they get it, they do not want it anymore."

_____

_____

_____

_____

_____

Making Matches

Match each set of bulleted sentences to a summary statement in the box.

• •

_____ 1. • The children groaned when we woke them so early.
• My wife brought a blanket to sit on the ground.
• The sun appeared over the treetops.
• It was a magnificent sight to see.

_____ 2. • This activity teaches responsibility and caring for others.
• Limited space is needed to raise rabbits.
• Raising rabbits is an excellent way to learn about caring for pets.
• Children also form close bonds with these animals.

a. Having a garden can be very time consuming.
b. Raising rabbits is a valuable experience for children.
c. Torch is a very popular band.
d. This year's vacation to the amusement park was lots of fun.
e. The new lasagna recipe was a hit with the whole family.
f. The sunrise my family experienced was spectacular.

_____ 3. • We arrived at the gates before the park opened.
• The weather stayed cool and sunny all day long.
• We rode every ride without having to wait in long lines.
• The roller coaster was the one we enjoyed the most.

_____ 4. • Dad spent three hours preparing lasagna for dinner.
• Mom kept opening the saucepan and sampling the sauce.
• All six of us had two helpings of lasagna.
• There were no leftovers to freeze for lunches.

_____ 5. • Tadas carefully laid out a plan for each section of his garden.
• The garden store where he bought supplies was very crowded.
• It took five days to prepare the plot and plant sunflower seeds.
• Tadas weeds his garden every Saturday morning.

_____ 6. • People were waiting in line for tickets all night.
• Fans of the band, Torch, were willing to pay $100 a ticket.
• The performance had the highest attendance in this stadium.
• Tickets for the concert sold out in less than two hours.

Name _____

Read the poem and answer the questions below.

I have planted a memory tree,
neither too great
nor too small.
A tree for life,
to celebrate the beauty around me
and to remind me.

May this tree of life I have set to earth
grow roots strongly anchored,
grow branches stretching wide,
to remind me often
of a grandparent's arms
and that loving embrace.

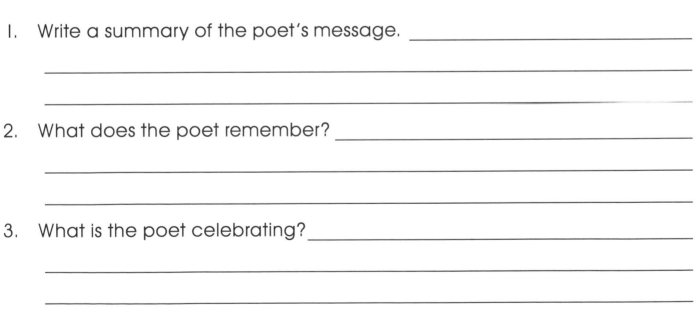

1. Write a summary of the poet's message. _____

   _____

   _____

2. What does the poet remember? _____

   _____

   _____

3. What is the poet celebrating?_____

   _____

   _____

4. Which word is a synonym for *secured*?_____

5. Which words show the poet is joyful? _____

   _____

Name _____

Puppy Love

Read the poem below. Then answer the questions.

My owner is the very best,
She pets and plays and all the rest.
I get the best food in my dish,
She is kinder than I'd ever wish.
I'd never put her to the test.

She loves me true, all of the time.
Even with a coat covered in grime.
Of course, there are times that she scolds,
But I am never left out in the cold.
Her love knows no reason or rhyme.

Even as we both grow up
And I am no longer just a pup,
She will still play and talk to me.
I know two friends we will always be,
Because she is the very best, yup!

1. Which detail should be included in a summary of this poem?

   a. The dog often gets covered in grime.

   b. The dog likes to eat yummy food.

   c. The dog thinks her owner is the best.

2. Which detail should not be included in a summary of this poem?

   a. The dog and her owner will both grow up one day.

   b. The dog likes spending time with her owner.

   c. The owner takes good care of her dog.

3. Name four things the dog loves about her life.

   _____

   _____

4. Using details from the poem, write a summary.

   _____

   _____

Summarizing • CD-104561

Name_____

Read the passage. Write a summary that includes all of the underlined words from the passage.

• •

Long ago, the northern forests in North America were not good for farming. The early <u>American Indians</u> who lived there hunted and fished for <u>food</u>.

To learn how to survive this way, they played <u>games</u> when they were young. Their games taught them all of the things they needed to know to become <u>hunters</u> and fishermen. For example, they needed to be able to pick up clues and signs from their environment. They played tracking games. They also needed to learn how to conceal themselves among trees, plants, and rocks, so, they played hiding games. In one game, young men threw axes. In another, they took turns throwing spears or sticks into a hoop on the ground. These games improved their accuracy. All of these activities helped them learn how to fish and hunt for food.

As the boys grew into fishermen, they used nets, traps, and spears to fish. With these <u>tools</u>, they caught whitefish and jackfish in lakes. In the rivers, they fished for Arctic grayling and trout. Meanwhile, hunters searched for moose, rabbits, and wolverines.

Young American Indians also had to learn how to adjust to the changing <u>seasons</u>. Hunters and fishermen used different techniques in the summers and winters. During the summers, <u>fishermen</u> caught food from the shores or in canoes. In the winters, they fished through holes cut into the ice. Sometimes, a hunter would discover a hibernating bear in the wintertime. That could feed a camp for several days.

When food became <u>scarce</u>, early American Indians lived on dried meat and fish. They also ate pemmican, a mixture of dried berries, dried meat, and animal fat.

_____

_____

_____

_____

_____

_____

Name_____

How Do We See?

Read an explanation of how the human eye sees. Answer the questions.

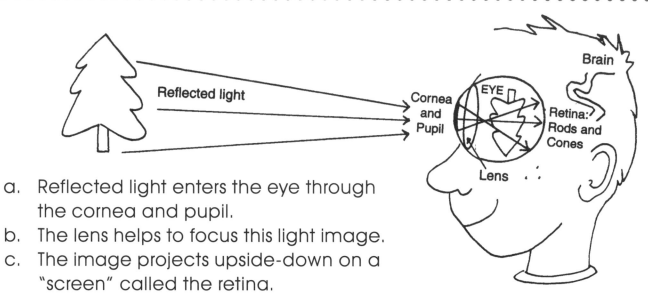

a. Reflected light enters the eye through the cornea and pupil.

b. The lens helps to focus this light image.

c. The image projects upside-down on a "screen" called the retina.

d. The retina has cones which distinguish color, light, and detail. These cones are especially useful for daytime vision. They send information to the brain by way of the optic nerve.

e. The retina also has rods which distinguish motion and objects. These rods are very important for nighttime vision. They also send information to the brain via the optic nerve.

f. A person has 20/20 vision if he sees at 20 feet what a person with normal vision can see at 20 feet. A person with 20/200 vision sees at 20 feet what a person with normal vision sees at 200 feet.

1. Summarize how we receive sight. _____

_____

_____

2. What does it mean to have 20/80 vision? _____

_____

_____

3. What does it mean to have 40/20 vision? _____

_____

_____

Name _____

Read this time line showing important dates in the life of Charles Conrad, Jr. Then answer the questions below.

1930	born in Philadelphia
1953	graduated from Princeton University
1953	entered Navy; completed Navy test for pilot school
1962	became an astronaut
1965	piloted the *Gemini 5* mission
1966	commanded the *Gemini 11* mission
1969	commanded the *Apollo 12* flight; landed module on the moon
1973	served as commander of the first mission of *Skylab*
1974	retired from both Navy and astronaut program

1. Write a simple summary of the life of Charles Conrad.

   _____

   _____

   _____

2. When did Conrad first become an astronaut? _____

3. In what year did he land on the moon? _____

4. For how many years did he serve in the Navy? _____

5. Which program came first: *Apollo, Gemini,* or *Skylab?* _____

Pasteur

Read the passage. Circle the answer to each question.

• •

A famous chemist named Louis Pasteur changed the way scientists think about disease. Pasteur was born in 1822 in Dole, France. He was a doctor of science but not a physician. As a result, many people in the medical profession did not take his work seriously. Pasteur wanted others to know that germs exist and that they cause disease. Eventually, he discovered a cure for a silkworm disease. He also developed vaccines for rabies and anthrax.

Pasteur also changed the way we drink milk. He developed a process called pasteurization. He created it as a way to remove germs from wine and beer. This process, called pasteurization after Pasteur, was later used to make milk safe to drink. During pasteurization, liquid is heated to kill any bacteria it contains. But heat cannot be too high, because it could change the taste of the milk.

To pasteurize milk, it must be heated to 140°F (60°C) for 30 minutes. The milk is then cooled quickly and sealed in sterile containers. That gets rid of the germs and preserves the taste.

In his later years, the importance of Pasteur's work was recognized by the medical community. He was often invited to speak at international medical meetings.

Each time you drink a glass of cold, refreshing, germ-free milk, you have Louis Pasteur to thank. And do not cry if you spill it! Milk is pasteurized each day. So, there is plenty more where that came from.

1. Which statement best describes Louis Pasteur?
   a. He was a doctor of science with an interest in medicine.
   b. He was a chemist who did not like medical doctors.
   c. He was a scientist who did not know much about diseases.

2. What is Pasteur best known for?
   a. drinking milk to stay strong and healthy
   b. speaking at medical meetings
   c. determining that disease is caused by germs

3. What is the best summary for this passage?
   a. Pasteur developed a vaccine for rabies.
   b. Pasteur developed the process of pasteurization.
   c. Pasteur developed a cure for all diseases.

A Picture-Perfect Moment

Read the cartoon, then answer the questions.

1. Which of the following best summarizes the cartoon?

   a. A father lovingly pushes his daughter on a swing.

   b. A father hurts his head while swinging his daughter.

   c. A daughter learns to swing for the first time.

2. Which detail should be included in a summary of this cartoon?

   a. A mother takes out a new camera to take pictures.

   b. A father performs a trick while swinging his daughter.

   c. A daughter does not like being pushed on a swing.

3. What does the word *underdog* mean in this cartoon?

   _____

4. Write a new title for this cartoon.

   _____

17

Wide World of Animals

Read the passage. Complete the activity on the next page. Use at least three words from the Word Bank to write a two-sentence summary for each animal.

• •

Uncle Bob loves animals. He has created a computer library of the animals that he likes the best. Here is information about three of his favorites.

Dolphins

These ocean-dwelling mammals live around the world. Dolphins have excellent hearing. They can hear noises at higher frequencies than humans can hear. Dolphins eat fish. They find food using their built in sonar, or echolocation. To do this, they make clicking noises underwater. These noises create sound waves that bounce off objects and echo back, which helps dolphins track and locate prey. A group of dolphins is known as a pod. Scientists consider these creatures to be among the most intelligent of all animals.

Baboons

These primates live in parts of Africa and Arabia. They prefer life on the ground to the tree climbing life of their cousins, the monkey. Their appearance makes them easy to identify. Baboons have long faces, overhanging brows, and colorful, hairless backsides. They eat small mammals, crustaceans, insects, and other tiny crawling creatures. They also feed on plants and fruit. One kind of baboon grazes on grass. Baboons have large cheek pouches that they use to store food. A group of baboons is called a troop. The size of a troop can range in number from 30 to 100.

Squirrels

Squirrels are considered rodents. They can be found in all parts of the world, except Australia and Antarctica. All but ground squirrels live in trees. They differ from one another in size. The pygmy squirrel of Africa is about the size of a hand, while the giant squirrel of Asia can grow up to 3 feet tall (91.44 cm). Squirrels love to eat buds, seeds, and nuts, but often will feast on insects. They have long front teeth that never stop growing, so they do not wear out from a lot of gnawing. Squirrels help trees and other plants grow by scattering and storing seeds.

Name _____

Word Bank			
animal	mammal	echolocation	rodent
food	pouches	primate	tree

Dolphins

_____

_____

_____

Baboons

_____

_____

_____

Squirrels

_____

_____

_____

Does It Fit?

The sentences below are details that fit one of these four summaries. Match the summaries to the supporting sentences. Write the correct letter for each summary on the blank lines.

Summary A: A young wolf roams the woods on her own for the first time.
Summary B: A girl plans a surprise family picnic.
Summary C: The city of Minneapolis has a bustling night life.
Summary D: A boy prepares for his first summer job.

_____ 1. When night falls, the streets fill with people who are eager to enjoy what the city has to offer.

_____ 2. At dawn, the young wolf decided to step out on her own.

_____ 3. He grabbed his uniform out of the dryer and hung it carefully on the hanger.

_____ 4. She pulled the cooler out of the garage and wiped it clean.

_____ 5. It was scary to be out in the woods all alone, but it was exciting too!

_____ 6. He showered and then shaved the few stray hairs growing on his young face.

_____ 7. At concerts, people listen to the music they enjoy.

_____ 8. She found apples and grapes in the refrigerator and rinsed them off.

_____ 9. At theaters, crowds line up to buy tickets to the newest plays.

_____ 10. She rummaged through the linen closet and found a picnic blanket.

_____ 11. She could hear the wind whistle through the trees and the birds singing from the branches as she walked past on her four paws.

_____ 12. He put on the clean uniform and combed his hair.

_____ 13. She packed sandwiches, fruit, cheeses, and pies, then called her family together to share her surprise.

_____ 14. As he walked to the burger stand, he imagined receiving his first paycheck.

Summarizing • CD-104561

Into the West

Read the passage. Write an outline to summarize the passage.

• •

The Shoshoni are an American Indian people. They live in the western part of the United States. Currently, their population numbers about 10,000 people. Long ago, this group traveled the western mountains and valleys. They moved with the seasons to find food. Today, many of them live on reservations.

The Shoshoni believed in a creator god. According to legend, he heard the morning prayer of the people. It lifted to heaven on the rays of the sun. The animals helped the god with his creations. The Shoshoni believed that Coyote made humans.

Hundreds of years ago, there was a Shoshoni woman named Sacagawea. She traveled with Lewis and Clark. She helped them speak with other American Indians. She also helped them find food. She taught them about the western environment too. When their boat capsized, she saved Clark's journals.

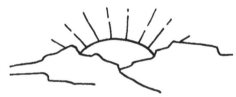

The presence of the young woman and her infant son helped ensure peaceful travel. Other American Indians trusted them. After all, if Lewis and Clark were planning to fight, they would not bring a woman and child with them.

Today, Sacagawea's face appears on a dollar coin. She and the Shoshoni people are an important part of American history.

The Shoshoni People of America

   I. _____

  II. _____

 III. _____

 IV. _____

  V. _____

 VI. _____

Name _____

Mystery of the Disappearing Lunches

Read the passage. Answer the questions below.

• •

As soon as we were old enough, we each became responsible for packing our own lunches. My five brothers made all of their lunches and I did, too. But having five brothers in the kitchen every morning equals chaos! I started making my lunch the night before when things were calm and quiet.

One Sunday night, I made my favorite lunch and stored the bag in the refrigerator. When I went to grab it on Monday morning, it was gone! Mom asked all of the boys, and each one denied taking my lunch.

I would have let it go, but the next morning, my lunch was missing again. Every day for a week, I had to make lunch in a rush because the one I had prepared the night before was gone.

My brothers can be annoying sometimes, but they are always honest. Mom wanted to believe them, but she also wanted to find out what was happening. She decided to talk to Dad about it. She had been trying not to bother him with too many problems because he had been working a lot of overtime hours lately. But, this was becoming increasingly frustrating. Should she ground all of the boys? Should she just give me lunch money?

Mom told Dad about the situation that night at the dinner table while we all sat eating. I was astonished to see Dad blush a little! Dad cleared his throat and then said, "Oh, that lunch wasn't meant for me? I thought you were saving me time by packing mine, since I've been leaving at five in the morning." Who could have guessed that Dad was the culprit? Our mouths dropped open in shock for a moment. Then, we all burst out laughing!

The mystery of my missing lunches was solved. Mom offered to make Dad his lunch on the days he worked overtime and my brothers were off the hook.

1. Use the details in the story to write a brief summary. Put events in sequential order.

    _____

    _____

    _____

    _____

2. Create another title for this story.

    _____

Name _____

A Dirty Deal

Read the letter and answer the questions.

• •

42 Current Ave.
Howell, MI 48843
February 12, 2000

Dear Sir or Madam,

Last fall, I purchased your much publicized video game, *Jungle Adventure.* In your television commercials, you claim that this game would put you "in the middle of a jungle."

First, the package arrived late. I ordered it online on October 5, but it did not arrive until December 4, well past the five-day delivery guarantee. Second, the game did not produce the sounds of slurping mud or sliding quicksand that was described in your commercials. Third, every time the hero makes it safely to the Monkey's Mambo on level four, the game freezes.

Finally, last Tuesday, the game caused a meltdown of my entire gaming system. I was entering a cave I discovered, not far from the Mud Monkey's Lair, when the screen became wavy. A text frame appeared reading, "Got You, Dirt Bag!" Fifteen seconds later, smoke poured out of my gaming system and it was completely broken.

Since I lost everything, I request two things of you. The first is a reimbursement for the game. The second is a down payment toward the purchase of a new gaming system.

With Dismay,
Jack Dram

1. Which of these statements best summarizes the intent of the letter?
    a. A buyer wishes to congratulate a company for keeping to its product.
    b. A buyer wishes to return a game that failed to meet expectations.
    c. A buyer wishes to receive money for a video game that was faulty.

2. What are the four complaints of the letter writer?
    a. _____
    b. _____
    c. _____
    d. _____

Ships of the Desert

Read the passage. Write a summary that includes all of the underlined words from the passage.

• •

Camels were once wild animals in Arabia and Asia. But, long ago they became domesticated. People of the desert began to use them to travel from one place to another. They also used them to transport things. Camels were the perfect animal for this job because they can carry heavy loads. They can also walk and run for a long time without needing to eat or drink.

There are two kinds of camels, the one-humped Arabian camel and the two-humped Bactrian camel. Both kinds can carry heavy loads. However, the Bactrian camel is sturdier. It can also withstand cooler climates. Arabian camels have shorter hair than the Bactrian camels. Because they only have one hump, they are more likely to be trained for racing.

A camel's hump is made of fat. The animal can use it for food when plants are not available on long desert walks. Camels also store water in their body tissues or in pouches inside their stomachs. The pouches help camels survive as they travel across the dry desert.

Nomadic people in North Africa and Asia still use camels. Their camels carry loads in areas where there are no roads.

Camels are called "ships of the desert" because of their swaying motion when they walk. Among the desert dunes, they look kind of like rocking ships on a sandy sea.

_____

_____

_____

_____

_____

Name _____

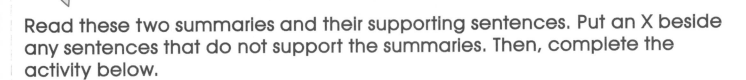

The Natural World

Read these two summaries and their supporting sentences. Put an X beside any sentences that do not support the summaries. Then, complete the activity below.

. . . .

1. A dragonfly prepares for flight and obtains food.
    _____ a. Spying a mosquito, the dragonfly flew over to snatch a meal.
    _____ b. A blue jay spotted the dragonfly below and cried out.
    _____ c. The insect lifted and swooped over the river's water in search of food.
    _____ d. The dragonfly fanned mist off its wings, drying them in the sun's light.
    _____ e. Dragonflies may be red, black, blue, or green.
    _____ f. As it continued its flight, the dragonfly ate its food.

2. The American mink is a skilled hunter.
    _____ a. The mature American mink may grow up to 20 inches (50 cm) in length.
    _____ b. A mink establishes his or her territory near rivers, streams, lakes, and marshes where it is easy to find prey.
    _____ c. Minks have a superb sense of smell that helps them track rabbits and squirrels.
    _____ d. The fox searched for food, which included mink, squirrel, and bird eggs.
    _____ e. Minks also have an extraordinary swimming ability, which helps them catch fish.
    _____ f. Two layers of fur protect minks living in cold climates and keep them warm.

Write four supporting sentences that support the following summary:
   The sunrise was the most beautiful thing he had ever experienced.

   a. _____
   b. _____
   c. _____
   d. _____

Name_____

Read the passage. Complete the activity on page 27.

• •

Dwight D. Eisenhower was born in Texas in 1890. Nicknamed "Ike," he served in the military for more than 30 years. During that time, he became a great leader. His efforts during World War II earned him respect around the world. His military career also prepared him to serve as president of the United States.

Ike grew up in a small town. There he learned the value of hard work, honesty, and self-reliance. Ike attended the military academy at West Point. After graduation in 1915, he began his career. Soon, he became a first lieutenant in the army. He worked on the staffs of great generals, such as Fox Conner and Douglas MacArthur. While serving as MacArthur's aide in the Philippines, he planned the Philippine military defense and helped in organizing a military academy for its newly formed independent country.

Shortly before the United States entered World War II, Eisenhower was promoted. He began serving in the war plan division. He did such as a good job that he was promoted again. Ike earned the title of major general. Later, he became the commanding general of U.S. forces in Europe. By 1943, he was promoted to a four-star general. That was the highest rank in the army at that time.

Under Ike's command, the Allied forces made plans to push the Germans out of France. Their greatest effort came on June 6, 1944. On that day, known as D-Day, Allied forces landed on the beaches of Normandy, in France. This invasion marked an important turning point. In less than a year, the Allies won the war in Europe.

In December of 1944, Ike was promoted to the new grade of five-star general. After the war ended, he continued to work in the military. He was named the Army Chief of Staff. Later, he was appointed as supreme commander of NATO forces in Europe.

Eisenhower remained in that position until he was nominated for president. His campaign slogan was "I Like Ike." In 1952, he was elected the 34th president of the United States. Ike served for two terms in the White House.

Name _____

I Like Ike (cont.)

1. Briefly summarize Eisenhower's military career. Write facts in sequential order.

   _____

   _____

   _____

   _____

2. List six military positions named in the passage that Eisenhower held.

   _____

   _____

3. Use dates from the passage to make a timeline of Eisenhower's life and career.

   _____

   _____

   _____

   _____

   _____

   _____

NASCAR Racing

Read the passage and fill in the outline on the next page. Draw a picture of a NASCAR race track in the box.

• •

The first automobile race took place in 1936 at Daytona Beach in Florida. More races followed and they were soon taking place throughout the South. But, the races were not organized. Many race tracks were makeshift. They were set up at county fairs for one race and taken down when the race was over. As a result, each race had its own rules.

Other tracks were permanent, but were not ideal. Some could handle the race cars. Some could handle the crowds who wanted to watch racing. But, very few tracks could handle both.

A driver and promoter named Bill France, Sr. thought that system did not work very well. He believed that drivers would have better races if there were better, more organized tracks. He also thought that drivers could earn bigger prizes if the rules were the same everywhere. He decided to make a change.

In 1948, France founded NASCAR, which stands for the "National Association for Stock Car Auto Racing." Stock car races are held on oval-shaped tracks. Drivers drive everyday cars that have been slightly modified for racing.

Over time, NASCAR became very popular. Race tracks were built throughout the country. The first asphalt race track was Darlington Raceway in South Carolina. Virginia's Richmond International Speedway was built five years after NASCAR was founded. The Lowe's Motor Speedway in North Carolina was the first track to hold night races.

The longest track is the Talladega Superspeedway in Florida. It is more than two miles around. The shortest track is Virginia's Martinsville Speedway. It is a little more than half a mile around. One of the most exciting races happens at the Bristol Motor Speedway in Tennessee. This track looks kind of like a big bowl. The lanes are very short and cars whip around and around them. All of these race tracks, along with many others, have played a part in NASCAR's history.

NASCAR drivers are known for their speed and skill. One of the greatest was Richard Petty. He came from a family of drivers and raced from 1958-1992. Dale Earnhardt, Sr. was another popular driver. During his career, he won 76 races.

NASCAR Racing (cont.)

NASCAR is now more popular than ever. It has about 75 million fans worldwide and its races are broadcast in over 150 countries. There are more than a hundred race tracks in the United States and Canada. NASCAR has also staged exhibitions in Japan, Mexico, and Australia.

The NASCAR Hall of Fame opened in 2010. Located in Charlotte, North Carolina, it is a place for fans to learn about the history of NASCAR. Exhibits show how racing changed from cars on dirt tracks to a sport watched all around the world.

The History of NASCAR

I. _____

II. _____

III. _____

IV. _____

V. _____

VI. _____

VII. _____

VIII. _____

What Is the Scoop?

Read the passage. Then, answer the questions on page 31.

• •

The world has enjoyed ice cream cones for more than 100 years. It is not entirely clear who invented the ice cream cone, although many people believe it was the creation of Italo Marchiony, an Italian immigrant in New York City.

In the early 1900s, Marchiony owned a pushcart. He used it to sell lemon ice on the sidewalks of New York. At the time, ice cream was sold by street vendors in small glasses. But, the glasses would sometimes break or customers would walk off with them accidentally. So, Marchiony decided to try something different. His first cone was made of paper. Then, he created an edible cone made from pastry. It became so popular that he applied for a patent for his edible cone.

Although Marchiony is credited with the invention of the cone, a similar creation was developed independently in 1904 at the St. Louis World's Fair. A vendor named Charles Menches had a stand there, where he sold ice cream in dishes.

One day at the fair, Menches ran out of dishes. It was very warm, and he still had several hours of business ahead of him. His friend Ernest Hamwi was selling a treat called zalabia. Zalabia was a crisp pastry sold with syrup. Menches asked his friend if he could borrow some of the zalabia. He rolled one up, scooped ice cream on top, and had an ice cream cone.

But no matter who invented the ice cream cone, it is still popular today. One scoop, two scoops, or even three, nothing beats eating ice cream from a cone.

What Is the Scoop? (cont.)

1. Which of the following best defines the word *patent*?
   a. a smooth leather
   b. a contract to buy on loan
   c. a loose-leaf notebook
   d. a right or license to make a product

2. Which provides the best explanation for the development of Menches' cone?
   a. He was trying to help out his friend Ernest Hamwi.
   b. He knew people would love ice cream in a cone.
   c. He ran out of dishes to serve ice cream.
   d. He had sold lemon ice this way for years.

3. Which of these statements is true?
   a. Marchiony sold ice cream in St. Louis.
   b. Hamwi sold ice cream in New York City.
   c. Menches sold lemon ice on the streets of New York City.
   d. Menches' cone was invented at the World's Fair.

4. Use your answers to the three questions to write a short summary for this passage.

   _____

   _____

   _____

   _____

Kids and Veggies

Read the passage. Then, answer the questions on page 33.

• •

How many servings of vegetables should children eat? Experts tell us that kids over the age of six should consume the same amount of vegetables as adults. That means kids should eat at least three servings per day, although, they would be better off with five servings.

Recent guidelines published by the Department of Agriculture suggest that fruits and vegetables should make up half of your plate at each meal. How can parents persuade their children to eat more vegetables? Here are some suggestions:

— Offer children raw veggies. Cooked vegetables sometimes taste bitter to children. However, raw vegetables do not have that bitter taste. Crunchy, raw vegetables can also be more appealing than overcooked veggies.

— Use low-fat dips or salad dressings with vegetables to make them more fun for kids.

— Encourage by example. Children need to see their parents eating vegetables on a daily basis. If they see how much their parents enjoy vegetables, they will like theirs too.

— Guide younger children into a routine. Tell them they must eat their vegetables before they can have their favorite foods.

— Mix vegetables in with other foods to encourage kids to eat more vegetables. It just makes good sense!

Name _____

1. Which detail should be included in a summary of this passage?

    a. Fruits taste much better than vegetables.

    b. Kids should be encouraged to eat more vegetables.

    c. No one enjoys eating vegetables.

2. Which detail should be included in a summary of this passage?

    a. Eating five servings of vegetables a day is ideal.

    b. People like to eat proteins and grains more than vegetables.

    c. Everyone should think about what they put on their plates.

3. Which detail should not be included in a summary of this passage?

    a. There are tips that can help parents encourage kids to eat vegetables.

    b. Children are more likely to eat raw veggies than overcooked vegetables.

    c. The Department of Agriculture keeps track of who likes to eat what.

4. Use your answers to the first three questions to write a summary about the passage.

    _____

    _____

    _____

    _____

Name _____

Blink of an Eye

Read the passage. Then, answer the questions on page 35.

• •

Blinking is the opening and closing of the eyelid. The average person blinks once every four seconds. That is about 15 times per minute during the waking hours of every day. So when you think about it, the average person blinks about 15,000 times each day! And it all happens automatically.

Eyelids are folds of skin that are raised and lowered by muscles. The lids of our eyes move much like the windshield wipers in a car. However, they move very quickly so our vision is not impaired. But, why do we blink, and why is blinking so important?

For one thing, blinking helps protect our eyes. Most of the eye is enclosed in a bony socket covered with a protective layer of fat. But, a part of the surface area becomes exposed when the eyes open. Eyelashes help keep dust and other particles out. However, sometimes they still get into the eye. Blinking helps remove irritants to keep the eyes from becoming damaged. If you start blinking fiercely, it probably means you have something in your eye.

Blinking also keeps the eyes lubricated. Along the edge of each eyelid are several tiny tear glands. They are located in between eyelashes. Every time an eyelid blinks, the glands release fluid. A film of tears coats the eye and prevents it from becoming too dry.

Have you ever had your picture taken and your eyes started to blink rapidly? That is because blinking also protects the eyes from bright lights. You may also blink more when cutting fresh onions. The onions release a gas that makes the eyes tear up and blink. When smoke gets into your eyes, that can make you blink more too.

There are also emotional reasons for why we blink. Our eyes tend to blink more during times of anxiety or stress than when we are calm. But, we tend to blink less when we are busy concentrating on a difficult project. Fatigue, disease, and injury to the eye can also affect how much we blink and how often.

Summarizing • CD-104561

Blink of an Eye (cont.)

1. Choose a new title for this passage.

   a. The Parts of the Eye

   b. What Makes Us Cry

   c. Why Our Eyes Blink

2. Which of these statements is true?

   a. Blinking is done voluntarily.

   b. Blinking helps keep eyes from becoming damaged.

   c. Our eyelids blink several times during each minute when we are asleep.

   d. Blinking helps to prevent the eye from becoming too moist.

3. What is another way that blinking helps us?

   a. It helps to keep our personal thoughts to ourselves.

   b. It prevents us from seeing unpleasant things.

   c. It helps to keep others from knowing our nervousness.

   d. It keeps dust and other particles from entering the eye.

4. Use the title you selected and your answers to the two questions to write a short summary for this passage.

_____

_____

_____

_____

Name _____

Animal Lovers

Read the story. Complete the activities on page 37.

• •

Terrance and Tabitha had always loved animals. Even as young children, the twins would rescue hurt or lost creatures they found on the farm. They learned to take care of animals from their parents and the farm veterinarian. As they grew older, they continued to rescue animals, often housing them in their parents' barn until a home could be found. This went on for years, so that by the time the twins were ready to graduate from high school, the O'Kelley's had rescued over one hundred dogs, even more cats and kittens, and an assortment of birds and other animals.

Mr. and Mrs. O'Kelley were not exactly surprised when the twins came to them with a new and wonderful scheme.

"Tabby and I would like to make our animal rescue an official thing. We want to open a pet rescue shelter. We will take in stray animals and try to find their owners. If we can't, we will find them good homes," said Terrance. He went on, "We would like to use the empty side of the main barn. We have it all planned out."

"How will you afford to feed and care for these animals?" Mrs. O'Kelley asked. That was Tabby's area. She explained, "We plan to ask local pet shops and individuals to donate pet food. We also plan to collect cans for recycling. We would like to ask the kids at the local schools to collect cans, too. New pet owners will pay an adoption fee that will help cover some of the costs of caring for their new pet."

"But, what about school?" Mr. O'Kelley questioned. "You'll both be going to college in the fall."

"We know, but we're going to college in town," Tabitha replied. "Right," said Terrence. "We'll be close by and we'll care for the animals after classes. Plus, we plan to ask for volunteers from the veterinary college to help feed and care for the animals. With help, we should be able to run the shelter and keep up with our school work," said Terrance.

Dad had a question. "What about the animals that really need medical attention? How do you plan on paying Dr. Wong for checking them out? Taking in sick or injured animals can be dangerous, kids!"

"We've already talked to Dr. Wong. He agreed that this is a great idea. He's even willing to volunteer two hours a week, if we help him on Saturday mornings. All we have to do is clean out the four kennels he has at the office. We know how to do that, since we do it for our own animals, so it won't be a problem," explained Tabitha.

Animal Lovers (cont.)

Mr. and Mrs. O'Kelley looked at each other. Mom smiled and said, "Well, you two have certainly done your homework. Why don't you go outside and let your father and me talk about this? We'll tell you our decision later." The twins walked outside and sat on the dock by the pond. Swinging their legs above the water, Terrance and Tabitha talked about their dreams for a pet rescue center. By dinner time, their parents had reached a decision.

"Your father and I have discussed your proposal and called Dr. Wong. He feels the two of you are very capable of running this type of operation. Dr. Wong has faith that you will make wise decisions about handling injured or scared animals. Your safety is one of our big concerns. We know you are responsible, but this is a big undertaking. We don't want it to interfere with your education."

Dad continued, "If we let you try this, it's on a trial basis only, just for the summer months. Also, you cannot have more than six 'residents' at a time."

Tabitha and Terrance could not sit still any longer. They flew out of their chairs and hurled themselves at their parents, hugging them.

"You guys won't regret this," said Tabitha, as she sat down at the dinner table. "We won't let you down."

"We won't let the animals down, either," said Terrence.

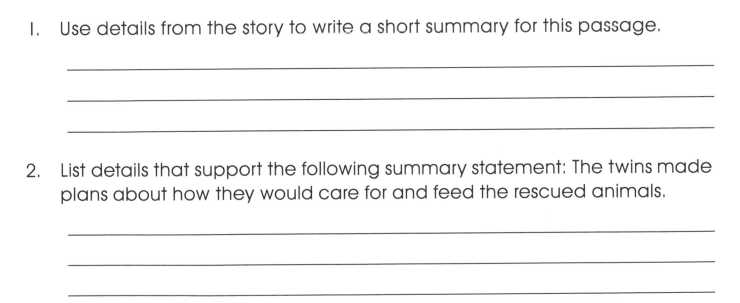

1. Use details from the story to write a short summary for this passage.

    _____

    _____

    _____

2. List details that support the following summary statement: The twins made plans about how they would care for and feed the rescued animals.

    _____

    _____

    _____

37

Name _____

Read the timeline. It highlights the career of an athlete named Babe Didrikson Zaharias. Then, answer the questions.

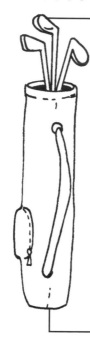

1914 Born in Port Arthur, Texas

1932 Won gold medals in the Olympics in track and field

1938 Married George Zaharias

1946 Won the U.S. Amateur Championship in golf

1949 Became a founding member of the Ladies Professional Golf Association

1950 Named by a poll as "the greatest woman athlete of the first half of the 20th Century"

1951 Won her fourth world championship in golf

1954 Won her final professional tournament, the U.S. Open

1955 Published her autobiography

1. Choose the sentence that best summarizes the timeline.

   a. Babe Didrikson Zaharias won gold in the Olympic for track and field.

   b. Babe Didrikson Zaharias showed what women can accomplish in sports.

   c. Babe Didrikson Zaharias was one of the greatest Texans who ever lived.

2. Which came first in Babe Didrikson Zaharias's life? Circle one.

   marriage   Olympics   U.S. Amateur Championship title

3. In which sport did Babe compete professionally?

   _____

4. What organization did Babe help found?

   _____

5. In what year did Babe publish her autobiography? Write your answer in a complete sentence.

   _____

Seeing Snakes

Read the passage. Circle the answer to each question.

• •

Snakes never close their eyes because they do not have eyelids. Instead, they have clear scales. When snakes shed their skin, they shed the scales over their eyes too.

Not all snakes have the same kind of vision. Some snakes have very keen eyesight, but others probably do not see color and can only distinguish between light and dark. Snakes that live in trees see more clearly than snakes that live under the ground. Many snakes have trouble seeing things that do not move.

Some snakes have eyes that help them to see at night and pits between their nostrils. These pits measure temperature and provide a kind of "heat vision." The snake's brain turns information about temperature into pictures. Having heat vision helps snakes hunt mice and rats in the dark.

1. What is this passage about?
   a. where snakes live
   b. how snakes move
   c. how snakes see

2. What is another possible title for this passage?
   a. Snake Eyes
   b. How Animals See
   c. Frogs and Snakes

3. What helps snakes hunt in the dark?
   a. clear eyelids
   b. nostril pits
   c. radar blips

4. What is the best summary sentence for this passage?
   a. Snakes see in different kinds of ways depending on where they live and how they survive.
   b. Some snakes live under ground, while others make their homes in the trees.
   c. Heat vision can often mean the difference between finding a meal and going hungry.

A New Jersey

Read the letter. Write the answer to each question.

• •

Dear Grandma,

    Thank you very much for the super-bright soccer jersey you bought for me. The pink and orange flowers make a very unusual pattern! The jersey is really big, too. Thank you for choosing a size I will not outgrow any time soon. Mom and I guess I will get at least four years of use out of the jersey.

    But unfortunately, I will not be able to wear it at Saturday's tournament. You see, our team colors are blue and yellow. I guess it is a league thing.

    I hope you visit soon! We would love to see you. Then you can come to a soccer practice or a game!

Love,
Madeleine

    P.S. Do not worry about buying more jerseys for the rest of the team. Ms. Diaz, the team's coach, wants to keep our current colors.

1.   Use details in this letter to write a summary. State the purpose of the letter in your summary.

    _____

    _____

2.   What are two of the problems with the jersey?

    _____

    _____

Downtown Traffic Flow Halted

Read the story. Write the answer to the each question.

• •

Traffic came to a halt Saturday morning. Everything suddenly stopped when the traffic light on the corner of Main Street went on the blink. By the time the county sheriff's department arrived, vehicles were backed up for several blocks.

Sheriff Wright said, "Must be the worst case of blockage we've seen in 23 years. Don't recall anything like it since the parade two summers ago."

The sheriff immediately deputized Debbie Dobson. He asked her to serve as traffic officer until electricity could be restored. Mrs. Dobson works as a school crossing guard. She has plenty of experience dealing with unruly traffic. "She did a great job," praised Betty Bunsen, a local store owner. "She kept traffic going as smooth as silk."

Four Corners Electric Company was able to restore power by the afternoon. Age and maintenance problems were blamed for the faulty wiring. Gabe Hoffman, a spokesperson for the FCEC, later gave a press conference. "If you want nice, new wires, you've got to get more money for maintenance. It's just that simple," he declared.

1. What is the purpose of this news article?

   _____

   _____

   _____

2. Use details from the story to write a short summary for this passage.

   _____

   _____

   _____

Headlines

Match each headline with the correct story. Then, complete the activity on page 43.

a. Bash Brings Out the Beasts in All
b. Peep Keeps Searching for Sheep
c. Clock Serves as Pest Control Device
d. Fifth-Grade Class—Mutton to Talk About
e. Webbed Wonder Frightens Girl
f. There Is Nothing That a Boy Will Not Get Into

_____ 1. The wooden grandfather clock was about to strike the hour of 1:00. A small rodent, seeking food, was scurrying up the front of the device. When the clock struck the hour, the tiny animal scampered away.

_____ 2. A prim and proper young lady was seated on a stool in her sitting room. She held a container of yogurt, which she spooned into her mouth ever so daintily. A spider lowered herself along a thread to have a look. The prim and proper young lady cried out and ran off.

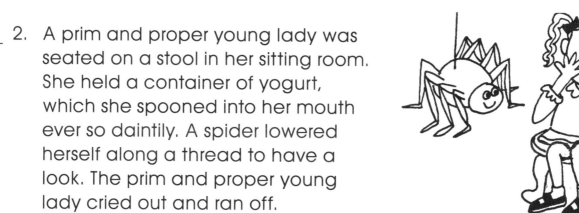

_____ 3. At the winter party, a curious young boy named Jack was sitting in a corner. This was due to mischief that he had caused earlier in the evening. When it was time for dessert, Jack was given a fruit tart to hold. Becoming curious, he decided to poke holes into the tart with his hands. He speared some of the fruit on one of his fingers. Noticing his mother's stern look, he cried out, "I'm a good little boy, right, Mommy?"

Headlines (cont.)

_____ 4. Miss Bo Peep works as a shepherdess from the north country. Recently, she misplaced her flock and was unable to locate them. After a long and difficult search, she was unable to find her sheep. Local authorities suggested she return home. They believe that the missing flock will soon follow her.

_____ 5. A young sheep followed its owner into her fifth-grade classroom today and disturbed the children. The students became increasingly excited and loud. As a result, the teachers will not permit any student to present his or her pet for weekly show-and-tell.

_____ 6. At Jan's summer party, everyone dressed in costumes. Dawn and Daniel dressed as a cow. They jumped over others, including Michael who had come as the Man-in-the-Moon. Hailey, in a dog costume, laughed so hard she held her sides with her hands. Other party goers included Pamela who dressed as a fiddle and Wayne who came as a cat.

43

Find Noah!

Read the story. Then, answer the questions on page 45.

• •

When Lamar came home from school he tossed his books on the table. "Noah, where are you boy?" he called, but his pet beagle did not come. As he opened the door of his mother's office a crack, she turned around. "Hi, Lamar, I didn't know you were home," she said.

"Have you seen Noah?" he asked. "No," she replied. "I let him out at lunchtime, but I thought I heard him come back in. You'll probably find him upstairs in your room asleep."

Lamar checked his room, but his dog was not there, so he searched the house from top to bottom and could not find Noah anywhere. When he told his mother, she was worried too. "I'll go outside and search," Lamar said. "Can you call the neighbors?" he asked. "Good idea," his mother answered, picking up the telephone.

Lamar walked down the street, calling at every driveway he walked past, "Noah, come on out boy." Soon, he saw neighbors from up and down the block climbing into their cars. When they drove by him, they waved and he could tell they were searching for Noah too.

Lamar searched for over an hour. He grew hungry and tired and his feet became very sore. Feeling hopeless, he decided to find out whether Noah had come back home on his own. As Lamar shuffled back to his house, he saw a crowd standing in his front yard from halfway down the block.

Lots of cars were parked in the middle of the street and people were standing around on the sidewalk. When Lamar drew closer, he noticed that a man he did not recognize had a dog that looked like Noah on a leash. Mrs. Sildano from the apartment building across the street was holding a beagle that looked like Noah in her arms. Mr. Chan from next door was telling a dog that looked like Noah to sit, while Jenny from the yellow house on the corner was tying a dog that looked like Noah to a fence post. That was an awful lot of beagles, and they all looked just like Noah!

His mother was standing on the porch and when she saw Lamar she began to frantically wave her arms. "Help, I don't know what to do!" she called. "Which one do you think is Noah?"

Summarizing • CD-104561

Find Noah! (cont.)

Just then, the real Noah emerged from a crawlspace under the house, where he had been taking a nap all afternoon. He yawned and stretched, then trotted over to each of the other Noahs and wagged his tail to be friendly. When Noah came to Lamar, he pawed the leg of his owner's jeans.

Lamar's mother invited the neighbors to a party that weekend to thank them for their help. They were all pleased that the real Noah was safe and sound, but they had to hurry to return the other beagles back where they found them.

1. The following sentences are details from the story. Decide which ones should be included in a summary of the story. Write *important* or *not important* on the line beside or below it.

    a. The real Noah emerged out of a crawlspace under the house.

    _____

    b. Lamar could not find his pet beagle when he came home from school. _____

    c. Lamar found his mother working in her home office. _____

    d. While Lamar went out to look for Noah, his mother asked the neighbors for help. _____

    e. Mrs. Sildano lives in an apartment building across the street.

    _____

    f. A man Lamar did not know stood beside a beagle that was on a leash. _____

    g. Lamar shuffled back to his house on his sore feet. _____

    h. The neighbors brought several dogs that looked like Noah to Lamar's house. _____

2. Use details from the story to write a short summary for this passage.

    _____

    _____

    _____

    _____

    _____

Answer Key

Page 4
Circle: 1. b; 2. c; 3. a

Page 5
Circle: 3

Page 6
Circle: Summary B

Page 7
Fill in the blanks: insects; chemicals; light; mate; hatch; adults

Pages 8–9
1. b; 2. a; 3. c; 4. d; 5. Answers will vary.

Page 10
1. f; 2. b; 3. d; 4. e; 5. a; 6. c

Page 11
1. A child plants a tree to help him deal with missing a grandparent. 2. his grandparent's love; 3. the beauty of the world and love; 4. anchored; 5. Answers will vary. Possible answers are: celebrate the beauty, loving embrace, and life.

Page 12
1. c; 2. a; 3. Possible answers: The dog loves the food she gets, the petting, the playing, and hugs from her owner; 4. Possible answer: From the dog's point of view, her owner will love and care for her no matter what.

Page 13
Answers will vary, but should include each underlined word from the passage at least once.

Page 14
1. Light travels into the eye where the lens focuses it. It is then projected onto the retina which sends this message (image) to the brain.
2. One sees at 20 feet what a person with normal vision sees at 80 feet.
3. One sees at 40 feet what a person with normal vision can only see at 20 feet.

Page 15
1. Charles Conrad, Jr. was an active participant in the United States space program. 2. 1962; 3. 1969; 4. twenty-one; 5. Gemini

Page 16
Circle: 1. a; 2. c; 3. b

Page 17
1. a; 2. b; 3. pushing a swing while holding the seat with both hands and running forward and under the swing seat; 4. Answers will vary.

Pages 18–19
Answers will vary. Dolphin summaries should contain the words *mammal* and *echolocation*. Baboon summaries should contain the words *primate* and *pouches*. Squirrel summaries should contain the words *rodent* and *tree*. All three summaries should contain the words *animal* and *food*.

Page 20
1. c; 2. a; 3. d; 4. b; 5. a; 6. d; 7. c; 8. b; 9. c; 10. b; 11. a; 12. d; 13. b; 14. d

Page 21
Answers will vary. Possible answers: I. native people of western United States; II. once traveled with the seasons; III. live on reservations today; IV. believed in a creator god; V. Sacagawea was a Shoshoni woman; VI. She helped Lewis and Clark.

Page 22
Answers will vary. Possible answers: 1. The lunches of an only daughter keep disappearing from the refrigerator. After a week, Mom steps in to figure out which of the five brothers is taking the lunch. Mom decides to call in Dad's advice. During dinner, Dad admits that he is the one taking the lunches. 2. Oh, Brothers!

Page 23
1. c; 2. a. package arrived late; b. audio was not good; c. game froze up; d. game caused meltdown of gaming system

Page 24
Answers will vary, but should include each underlined word from the passage at least once.

Page 25
Place an X beside: 1. b, d, and e; 2. a, d and f; Answers will vary.

Pages 26–27
1. Answers will vary. Possible answers are: Eisenhower began his military career at West Point. He quickly moved up in rank. He worked with such famous men as Fox Conner and Douglas MacArthur. Eisenhower was a part of major military situations, including Philippine independence and the battle at Normandy, during World War II. 2. first lieutenant, major general, four-star general, five-star general, Army Chief of Staff, and supreme commander. 3. Time line should include the six dates/years mentioned in the given passage.

Pages 28–29
Answers will vary. Possible answers:
I. Early racing was unorganized.
II. NASCAR was founded in 1948.
III. Race tracks were built over time.
IV. NASCAR became very popular.
V. There are different kinds of tracks.
VI. Drivers have speed and skill.
VII. NASCAR has millions of worldwide fans today.
VIII. The Hall of Fame opened in 2010. Drawings will vary, but should show a race track.

Pages 30–31
1. d; 2. c; 3. d; 4. Answers will vary.

Pages 32–33
1. b; 2. a; 3. c; 4. Answers will vary, but should include details chosen from the first three questions.

Pages 34–35
1. c; 2. b; 3. d; 4. Answers will vary.

Pages 36–37
Answers will vary.

Page 38
1. b; 2. Olympics; 3. golf; 4. Ladies Professional Golf Association; 5. She published her autobiography in 1955.

Page 39
Circle: 1. c; 2. a; 3. b; 4. a

Page 40
1. A granddaughter thanks her grandmother for a soccer jersey given as a gift. 2. colors are wrong and much too large

Page 41
Answers will vary. Possible answers:
1. The article was written to inform the public about recent traffic problems. 2. Poor traffic light wiring caused problems on Saturday.

Pages 42–43
1. c; 2. e; 3. f; 4. b; 5. d; 6. a

Pages 44–45
1. a. important; b. important; c. not important; d. important; e. not important; f. not important; g. not important; h. important; 2. Answers will vary, but should include only the important sentences.